Rollicking Rhymes

BY CAITIE MCANENEY

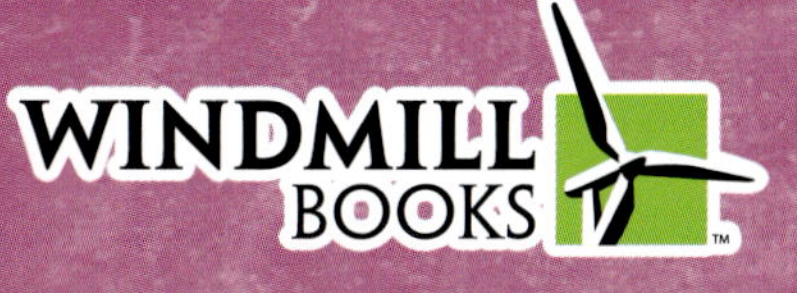

WINDMILL BOOKS

Published in 2025 by Windmill Books, an Imprint of Rosen Publishing
2544 Clinton St., Buffalo, NY 14224

First Edition

Editor: Caitie McAneney
Book Design: Claire Zimmermann

Photo Credits: Series art (illustrations) Huza Studio/Shutterstock.com; series art (purple painted background) elena_l/Shutterstock.com; cover (boy) jesadaphorn/Shutterstock.com; series art (interior biege background) Q3kiaPictures/Shutterstock.com; p. 5 (boy) AI Generated/Shutterstock.com; p. 5 (Mother Goose) fairo/Shutterstock.com; p. 6 (rat) MaxNadya/Shutterstock.com; p. 7 olgagorovenko/Shutterstock.com; p. 8 kichikimi/Shutterstock.com; p. 9 (girl) Arina P Habich/Shutterstock.com; p. 9 (ice skates illustration) Saramix/Shutterstock.com; p. 10 (squirrel) Callmebebak/Shutterstock.com; p. 11 (squirrel) Becky Sheridan/Shutterstock.com; p. 11 (nuts illustrations) wasapohn/Shutterstock.com; p. 13 Manop Boonpeng/Shutterstock.com; p. 15 Wirestock Creators/Shutterstock.com; p. 17 Jay Ondreicka/Shutterstock.com; p. 19 (canary photo) palagand/Shutterstock.com; p. 19 (bird illustration) Mei Yuan 27/Shutterstock.com; p. 21 Fordelse Stock/Shutterstock.com.

Some of the images in this book illustrate individuals who are models. The depictions do not imply actual situations or events.

Library of Congress Cataloging-in-Publication Data
Names: McAneney, Caitie, author.
Title: Rollicking rhymes / Caitie McAneney.
Description: Buffalo, NY : Windmill Books, 2025. | Series: Let's get silly!
  | Includes index.
Identifiers: LCCN 2024025326 (print) | LCCN 2024025327 (ebook) | ISBN
  9781538397992 (library binding) | ISBN 9781538397985 (paperback) | ISBN
  9781538398005 (ebook)
Subjects: LCSH: Rhyme–Juvenile literature.
Classification: LCC PN1059.R5 M37 2025 (print) | LCC PN1059.R5 (ebook) |
  DDC 811–dc23/eng/20240701
LC record available at https://lccn.loc.gov/2024025326
LC ebook record available at https://lccn.loc.gov/2024025327

Manufactured in the United States of America

CPSIA Compliance Information: Batch #CWWM25. For further information, contact Rosen Publishing at 1-800-237-9932

Contents

Words in the glossary appear in bold the first time they are used in the text.

What's a Rhyme?

If you've ever heard a **nursery rhyme** or song, you've likely heard plenty of rhyming. Words that rhyme usually have the same end sound, for example, "mine" and "fine." Near rhymes have almost the same sound, but a little different. For example, "mine" and "lion." You can use rhyming to make up some silly jokes, stories, and songs!

Fun Fact

Mother Goose is said to be the author of many nursery rhymes. No one knows if Mother Goose was a real person.

Silly Animals

There once was a dog on a log.
The dog said hello to a frog.
The frog jumped down, then looked around,
and said, "Hey, quit hogging my log!"

HA!

Mattie Blatt wanted a cat,
but he could only afford a rat.
The rat, named Pat, sat down to chat.
He said, "Now, can a cat do that?"

Fun Fact

Rats are very smart animals! They can be trained to do tricks and count.

Play All Day

Paul McCall was eight feet tall.
He worried he had no talents at all.
Until one day someone asked Paul,
"Have you ever tried out for basketball?"

Fun Fact

The tallest players in NBA history were Gheorghe Muresan and Manute Bol. They were both 7 feet 7 inches (2.3 m) tall.

Katie Lates was a whiz on skates.
She could do flips and figure eights.
She jumped plates and crates and even gates,
and her name went down with the greats.

POemS with a PUnch

There once was a squirrel named Earl
who sold all his nuts for a pearl.
Winter set in, and Earl was grim,
for pearls cannot feed a squirrel.

HEEHEE!

This hotel is run by a ghost.
In truth, she's a very poor host.
She'll burn your toast
and hide the things you need most.
What did you expect from a ghost?

Fun Fact

Each squirrel can bury 3,000 nuts per season to survive the long winter!

School IS Cool!

Maisy Gray got straight A's.
She could read and write all day.
Her teachers finally had to say,
"Miss Gray, don't forget to play!"

Have you met old Mister Barts?
He teaches math and sometimes art.
He fingerpaints his graphs and charts,
and says, "Each child is smart at heart."

Fun Fact
Some experts say that kids should have playtime, especially
outdoors, for three or more hours a day!

Bugging Out

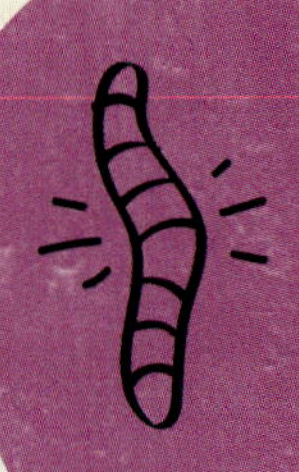

This is an **ode** to a worm named Rose
who glowed from her tail to her nose.
In this deep, dark cave, everyone knows:
If you need a light, just ask for Rose!

Grant the ant ate a whole plant,
though his anthill's stores were **scant**.
The other ants began to **rant**,
"That Grant never shares his plant!"

Fun Fact

Some glowworms are beetles. Others are fungus gnat larvae that live in caves. Their bodies make light, which is an example of **bioluminescence**.

Mark the shark had lost his bark.
No one feared him in the dark.
He opened his mouth, and fish remarked,
"Have you ever seen a toothless shark?"

How can you spot a beluga whale?
From top to bottom, its skin is pale.
It sports a big head and pure-white tail.
Keep an eye out when you sail!

Fun Fact

Great white sharks have about 300 teeth in their heads. When they lose one, another pops up in its place!

Royal Rhymes

Princess Pam was in a jam.
She lost the queen's favorite lamb.
She said, "Little Lamb, I have a yam!"
Little Lamb said, "Here I am!"

TEEHEE!

The King's canary would sing all spring,
but the King sold it for a ring.
Though he loved his shiny new bling,
he cried because it couldn't sing.

Fun Fact

Canaries are little yellow birds that have been kept as pets for hundreds of years. They are known for their beautiful singing.

Space Race

Casey and Chase entered a race
to see if they could get to space.
Said Chase, "I know nothing about the place.
Better pack some snacks, just in case!"

Lars the alien lived on Mars
but dreamed of visiting other stars.
"If only we had flying cars,
I know the universe could be ours."

No aliens have been found on Mars. However, billions of years ago, it may have been home to **microbes**.

Glossary

bioluminescence: Light given off naturally by certain kinds of insects, fish, or bacteria.

larvae: The stage of an insect's life after it hatches from an egg and before it changes into its adult form.

microbe: A tiny living thing that can only be seen with a microscope.

NBA: Short for National Basketball Association, a major U.S. sports league that organizes and regulates the highest level of men's basketball.

nursery rhyme: A short, simple, usually rhymed song or poem for young children.

ode: A long, usually rhymed lyrical poem, often in praise or celebration of something or someone.

rant: To speak or complain loudly.

scant: Very little.

For More Information

BOOKS

Edwards, Jonas. *Rhyme Time with Sharks!* New York, NY: Gareth Stevens Publishing, 2021.

McClure, Leigh. *Rhyme Time with Ants!* Buffalo, NY: Gareth Stevens Publishing, 2024.

Stasson, Anita. *Beet Street.* Minneapolis, MN: Bearport Publishing Company, 2024.

WEBSITES

How to Write a Traditional Nursery Rhyme
poetry4kids.com/lessons/how-to-write-a-traditional-nursery-rhyme/
Learn how to write your own nursery rhyme.

Popular Nursery Rhymes with Lyrics
allnurseryrhymes.com
Check out this collection of popular nursery rhymes to practice recognizing rhyming words.

Index